JACK THORNE

Jack Thorne's other plays for the stage include an adaptation of *Stuart: A Life Backwards* (Underbelly, Edinburgh and tour, 2013); *Mydidae* (Soho, 2012; Trafalgar Studios, 2013); an adaptation of Friedrich Dürrenmatt's *The Physicists* (Donmar Warehouse, 2012); *Bunny* (Underbelly, Edinburgh, 2010; Soho, 2011); *2nd May 1997* (Bush, 2009); *When You Cure Me* (Bush, 2005; Radio 3's Drama on Three, 2006); *Fanny and Faggot* (Pleasance, Edinburgh, 2004 and 2007; Finborough, 2007; English Theatre of Bruges, 2007; Trafalgar Studios, 2007); and *Stacy* (Tron, 2006; Arcola, 2007; Trafalgar Studios, 2007). His radio plays include *Left at the Angel* (Radio 4, 2007), an adaptation of *The Hunchback of Notre Dame* (2009) and an original play *People Snogging in Public Places* (Radio 3's Wire slot, 2009). He was a core writer in all three series of *Skins* (E4, Channel 4, BBC America), writing five episodes. His other TV writing includes *The Fades* (2012 BAFTA for Best Drama Series), *Shameless, Cast-Offs, This is England '86* (2011 Royal Television Society Award for Best Writer – Drama), *This is England '88, This is England '90* and the thirty-minute drama *The Spastic King*. His work for film includes the features *A Long Way Down*, adapted from Nick Hornby's novel, and *The Scouting Book for Boys*, which won him the Star of London Best Newcomer Award at the London Film Festival 2009.

Other Titles in this Series

LET THE
RIGHT ONE IN

Based on the novel and film by
John Ajvide Lindqvist

Adapted for the stage by
Jack Thorne

NICK HERN BOOKS
London
www.nickhernbooks.co.uk

A Nick Hern Book

This stage adaptation of *Let the Right One In* first published in Great Britain as a paperback original in 2013 by Nick Hern Books Limited, The Glasshouse, 49a Goldhawk Road, London W12 8QP

Reprinted 2014

Låt den rätte komma in (novel) copyright © 2004 John Ajvide Lindqvist, published in English as *Let Me In*, translation © 2007 Ebba Segerberg

Let the Right One In (stage adaptation) © 2013 Jack Thorne and Marla Rubin Productions Ltd

Jack Thorne has asserted his right to be identified as the author of this adaptation

Cover image: Manuel Harlan
Cover design: Ned Hoste, 2H

Typeset by Nick Hern Books
Printed in Great Britain by Mimeo Ltd, Huntingdon, Cambridgeshire PE29 6XX

A CIP catalogue record for this book is available from the British Library

ISBN   978 1 84842 412 8

Let the Right One In received its West End premiere at the
Apollo Theatre, London, on 7 April 2014 (previews from
26 March). Marla Rubin and Bill Kenwright presented a
National Theatre of Scotland production in association with the
Royal Court Theatre. The cast was as follows:

ELI	Rebecca Benson
JONNY	Graeme Dalling
HALMBERG/MR AVILA	Gavin Kean
KURT/JOCKE/NILS/DAD/ STEFAN	Gary Mackay
HAKAN	Clive Mendus
TORKEL/JANNE/JIMMY	Angus Miller
MICKE	Cristian Ortega
OSKAR	Martin Quinn
OSKAR'S MUM	Susan Vidler
UNDERSTUDIES	Jessica Bastick-Vines
	Mairi Cowieson
	Tom Gillies
	Padraig Lynch

Director	John Tiffany
Associate Director	Steven Hoggett
Designer	Christine Jones
Lighting Designer	Chahine Yavroyan
Sound Designer	Gareth Fry
Costume Co-Designer	Aileen Sherry
Special Effects	Jeremy Chernick
Music	Ólafur Arnalds
Resident Director	Justin Martin
Associate Movement Director	Vicki Manderson
Design Associate	Tim McQuillen-Wright
Casting	Anne Henderson

Let the Right One In was previously performed at the Royal Court Jerwood Theatre Downstairs, London, on 29 November 2013, with the following cast:

ELI	Rebecca Benson
JONNY	Graeme Dalling
KURT/JOCKE/NILS/DAD/ STEFAN	Paul Thomas Hickey
HALMBERG/MR AVILA	Stephen McCole
TORKEL/JANNE/JIMMY	Angus Miller
MICKE	Cristian Ortega
OSKAR	Martin Quinn
HAKAN	Ewan Stewart
OSKAR'S MUM	Susan Vidler

Let the Right One In was commissioned by the National Theatre of Scotland and Marla Rubin Productions Ltd, and first produced by the National Theatre of Scotland by arrangement with Marla Rubin Productions Ltd and Bill Kenwright, in association with Dundee Rep Theatre, at Dundee Rep Theatre on 5 June 2013.

Characters

OSKAR
JONNY
MICKE
HAKAN
TORKEL
KURT
MUM
ELI
HALMBERG
JOCKE
MR AVILA
NILS
DAD
JANNE
JIMMY
STEFAN

ACT ONE

Scene One

A man walks through the woods along a distinct path. He is
TORKEL. He's drunk but concentrating very hard on seeming
sober.

HAKAN emerges from the woodland in the opposite direction.
He stands looking at the man. HAKAN is wearing a rucksack
and in his hands he carries a gas cylinder. He thinks and then
withdraws from the light again.

As TORKEL walks past so HAKAN steps out in front of him.
TORKEL looks at HAKAN, who looks back with a steady
intensity.

TORKEL. Hiya... can I help...

> HAKAN *says nothing.*

> Do you want something?

HAKAN. The time.

TORKEL. Sure thing. The time is...

He checks his watch. HAKAN grabs the back of his head,
twists him and holds a gas mask to his face. TORKEL's legs
buckle beneath him. He slumps, unconscious.

And then HAKAN takes his rucksack off and begins tying
TORKEL's legs.

Scene Two

A boy, OSKAR, *runs into a locker room. He is in a PE vest, shorts and some daps. He opens his locker, grabs his school uniform inside and tries to get clothed as quickly as possible.*

JONNY. Pig-gy?

> OSKAR*'s face crinkles. His feet move up and down slightly. He's scared.*

MICKE. Hey, Piggy, are you in there?

> *There is a pause.*

Piggy, we know you're in there...

> OSKAR *looks around for means of escape – there are none – he opens the locker again. He climbs inside.*

> *Suddenly two dark figures crawl over the top of the lockers and look down on* OSKAR. *They are* MICKE *and* JONNY. *If not older than* OSKAR, *then certainly bigger and stronger.*

JONNY. Little Pig, if you don't come out now, we have to get you out of school? Is that what you want... Is that what you want, Little Pig?

MICKE. Don't make us hunt you, Little Pig...

JONNY. Don't make us blood you...

> *They jump down.*

MICKE. Pig-gy...

> *They open one locker.*

JONNY. Pig-gy...

> *They open another locker.*

BOTH. Pig-gy...

> *They open* OSKAR*'s locker.*

JONNY. Squeal like a pig, bitch.

MICKE. Squeal like a pig, bitch.

> OSKAR *squeals like a pig.*

The three boys wait and listen. Listen for if anyone's coming.

JONNY. No one's coming, bitch. Get ready to be baptised, bitch.

The two boys make to pull OSKAR out, and the light goes out.

Scene Three

We're in a sweet shop. Bright, colourful, strip-lit, and with strange piped-in music.

OSKAR stands looking at row upon row of sweets. He is in school uniform but his collar and jacket have been ruffled up.

He has a look on his face of quiet contemplation. He picks up a chocolate bar, kneels to do up his shoelaces and slips it into his sock. He then stands and looks back into the sweets.

KURT. Are you buying or are you just looking?

OSKAR turns, surprised to be being watched. KURT is in his mid-thirties and distrustful of children.

OSKAR. I'm choosing.

KURT. It's a bit late to be eating sweets.

OSKAR. Not so late.

KURT walks past him. OSKAR slips a packet of fruit gums into his pants.

I won't be long.

KURT looks at OSKAR carefully.

KURT. Is that blood on your shirt?

OSKAR. No.

KURT. Yes, it is, it's blood.

OSKAR. Maybe.

KURT looks at OSKAR carefully again.

KURT. Did someone do that to you?

OSKAR. No.

KURT. Did other boys do that to you?

OSKAR. No.

KURT. Are you okay?

OSKAR. Yes.

> OSKAR *slips a packet of cola drops into his shirt.*

I've decided.

> *He takes a lollipop up to the counter.*

KURT. This all you're having?

OSKAR. Yes. Sorry.

> *He takes some change from his pocket, he carefully counts it out.*

I like your lollies, they're tasty.

> *He nods at* KURT *and makes to leave.*

KURT. Kid…

> OSKAR *turns, scared he's been rumbled.*

OSKAR. Yes?

> KURT *throws him a chocolate bar.*

KURT. Be safe, kid.

OSKAR. Okay. I will be.

> OSKAR *leaves, with a smile on his face.*

Scene Four

HAKAN *attaches the rope to the man's ankles, tying them extremely carefully. He then removes the mask from around the man's face and, using the branch as a pulley mechanism, pulls the man up so that he's hanging from the branch.*

He then unpacks from his bag a plastic groundsheet, a container, a funnel and a knife. He begins to fastidiously spread out the plastic sheeting.

TORKEL. I don't...

HAKAN *pays no attention to him. He gets the jug and arranges it underneath the man.*

Where is – what is – this?

HAKAN *pays no attention. He puts the funnel into the jug. The man realises where he is.*

No... No... Don't do this. Please. Please. I have a baby.

HAKAN *pays no attention. The man starts to make strange noises. Noises of pure fear. He's not crying, he's not screaming, it's something far worse.*

HAKAN. Forgive me.

HAKAN *cuts* TORKEL's *throat. A gush of blood falls into the jug.*

And then suddenly torches blare through the woodland and the sound of lads playing.

HAKAN *looks around – they're coming straight for him – thoroughly panicked. He makes to run.*

He returns. He picks up the jug, the knife and the funnel. He drops the jug. He curses. He picks it up again. He runs off.

Scene Five

POLICE COMMISSIONER HALMBERG. The incident took place in the woods.

I cannot give you the name of the man killed, I can tell you we do believe it a murder.

It is the second such episode to occur within the past week. We have been unable to make close examination but it does look as if the cases may be linked.

I therefore ask all my fellow citizens to keep their vigilance and urge them to stay away from the woods at night unless absolutely necessary.

We will catch this killer but until we do you must stay safe.

Anyone with any information they feel could be useful – anything they saw or heard – the slightest thing – should dial the incident room, the number is on the screen.

No questions.

OSKAR *sits eating dinner with his* MUM *on a sofa. A sallow-faced, overwhelmed-looking woman.* OSKAR *is picking at a TV chicken dinner in a foil tray. His* MUM *is just drinking from a large glass of wine. The clock ticks loudly in the background.*

MUM. Not hungry?

OSKAR. Not really.

MUM. Filled up on sweets I imagine.

OSKAR. No.

MUM. You are not to go out to the woods, do you hear?

OSKAR. I don't go in the woods.

MUM. You're to stay close until they've caught him.

OSKAR. You don't want me to go to school?

MUM. Don't cheek me, Oskar. Of course you go to school. But then you come back here and stay on the estate. Until they've caught him.

OSKAR. What if they never catch him?

MUM. Do you want to be murdered? Is that it? Do you want to be butchered? Do you want me to sit here and have my door knocked on by a sad-looking fat policeman. Nothing can happen to you. If it does, I'd die too.

OSKAR picks up his knife and puts it in his pocket.

OSKAR. Okay. I'm going out.

MUM. Did you not listen to a word I said?

OSKAR. Just out into the courtyard.

MUM. I don't want you to go out into the courtyard.

OSKAR. Just for a little while.

His MUM *thinks.*

MUM. And nowhere else, do you hear?

OSKAR nods.

And don't forget your hat. It is cold. I don't want you getting a cold.

OSKAR. I won't, Mum.

Scene Six

And suddenly everything is gone…

And we're left with OSKAR *– a tree – and a weird piece of some sort of climbing apparatus. A jungle gym.*

OSKAR *is in a coat and a hat. He has his dinner knife with him. He blows out a breath of pure cold steam. He stabs the tree with a knife. And again. And a third time.*

OSKAR. What are you looking at?

He stabs again. He sounds unconvincing. But he's trying hard.

What are you looking at, you fucking – idiot?

And then ELI – *before now hidden from view – climbs up from the back end of the climbing apparatus so as to sit on the top. She's about the same age as* OSKAR *but, unlike him, wears no hat, gloves or coat. In fact, all she wears is a pink jumper, but she doesn't look cold. She also looks very unwashed – with lank, greasy hair.*

OSKAR *doesn't notice her and stabs the tree again.*

What are you looking at, you fucking idiot? You – bitch. Do you want to die?

He stabs again.

Do you want to die, bitch? That's what happens when you so much as look at me... bitch...

He stabs again and ELI *laughs.* OSKAR *looks up at her – surprised. He drops the knife.*

He picks the knife up again – he looks at the knife. He tries to tuck the knife into his trousers. It doesn't fit. He puts it back on the floor. ELI *smiles,* OSKAR *isn't sure what that means.* OSKAR *thinks and then scratches his nose.*

Hi.

ELI *says nothing.*

I said 'hi'.

ELI. I heard you.

OSKAR. Why didn't you answer?

ELI *shrugs.*

Aren't you cold?

ELI. What are you doing?

OSKAR. Practising.

ELI. For what?

OSKAR. For – if the murderer comes along...

ELI. What murderer?

OSKAR. You haven't heard about the murderer?

ELI. If I had I wouldn't be asking you, would I?

OSKAR. The one who killed those guys... Killed them like pigs.

ELI *sighs and looks up at the moon.*

They say he killed them like pigs. Hung them up and watched the blood drain. I'm not lying. Like a pig.

ELI. Yes.

OSKAR. Aye.

ELI. And that means – are you scared? Are you stabbing the tree because you're scared?

OSKAR *blushes.*

OSKAR. No, but a murderer, that's like... it's good if you can... defend yourself. Do you live here?

ELI. Yes.

OSKAR. Where?

ELI. Over there. We've just moved in. Next door to you.

OSKAR *looks at her – surprised.*

OSKAR. How do you know where I live?

ELI. I've seen you in the window before. When I've been down here – before.

ELI *jumps from the jungle gym and lands in front of OSKAR. It's an impressive jump and she lands perfectly.*

OSKAR. You're good at jumping.

ELI. You think so?

OSKAR. Do you practise?

ELI. No.

OSKAR. Do you do jumping at school?

ELI. No.

ELI *thinks.*

I can't be friends with you. Just so you know.

OSKAR. What?

ELI. Sorry. I'm just telling you how it is. Just so you know.

OSKAR. What makes you think I'd want to be friends with you? You must be pretty stupid.

ELI walks up to OSKAR.

ELI. Sorry. But that's how it is.

OSKAR sniffs the air.

What?

OSKAR. Is that – strange smell coming from you?

ELI. What strange smell?

OSKAR. The smell like... The smell of my dog Bruno – when his coat was wet. Before he died. Is it coming from you?

He sniffs the air.

ELI. I guess so.

OSKAR looks at her a moment. He rubs his nose.

OSKAR. Are you really not cold?

ELI. No.

OSKAR. Why not?

ELI considers this.

ELI. I guess I've forgotten how to be.

OSKAR. Okay.

OSKAR thinks.

I should go in now.

ELI. Why?

OSKAR. Because I promised my mum...

ELI. And is that important?

OSKAR. If I want her to let me come out again it is.

ELI. Why do you need her permission?

OSKAR. Why do you care? We're not going to be friends. Night.

ELI. Night.

OSKAR. Okay.

OSKAR *walks away.*

ELI *climbs up onto the jungle gym again.*

OSKAR *turns and looks at her.*

Then he turns back and starts walking again.

And when he turns back a second time to ELI – *well, she's gone.*

Scene Seven

HALMBERG *stands in front of school assembly.*

HALMBERG. We are aware that some of you children spend a lot of time around the woods. So I'm here today to say two things. One, please stay away, it isn't safe. I know – I have children myself – that sense of danger might make a trip to a murder site seem more exciting – but I assure you this is not a game. Secondly, I am here to ask you for information – if anyone saw anything, last night or on the 2nd November happening in and around those woods – you are to inform any of your teachers – who will bring the matter to my attention. We are starting to build a profile of this killer and we will find him, but with your help we may find him faster. You may be worried about giving this information; maybe you weren't supposed to be in the woods. Well, I tell you now, you will not get in any trouble, we simply need all the information we can get so we can get this killer caught. Evil only needs silence. Please don't be silent.

Scene Eight

OSKAR *sits in a sandpit in the school playground. He picks up a stone and throws it in. It produces a nice puff of sand.*

He likes this. He does it again. MICKE *approaches behind him. He stands a moment.*

MICKE. What you doing?

OSKAR. Nothing.

MICKE. Why are you in a sandpit?

OSKAR. Because I want to be in a sandpit.

Beat. In the background, JONNY *sees them talking, frowns and approaches.* OSKAR *throws another rock.*

MICKE. You don't help yourself, you know that…

OSKAR. I know.

MICKE. Oskar, just go…

OSKAR *turns just as* JONNY *reaches them.*

JONNY. Do you think this looks suspicious, Micke?

Both MICKE *and* OSKAR *freeze –* MICKE *doesn't turn around.*

MICKE. In what way?

JONNY. He is sitting in a kids' sandpit throwing rocks… He is too big for a sandpit. He's probably just here to look at the kids.

OSKAR. There are no kids here…

JONNY. Should we report it to the police, Micke?

MICKE. I would say we had to. I would say it was our duty.

JONNY. Little kids are supposed to play here, don't you know that, Piggy? Little kids who could get hurt by your rocks…

OSKAR. There are no kids here…

JONNY. They could cut their feet. Tell me that you're sorry, Piggy. Tell me you're sorry for cutting the little kids' feet.

OSKAR. I can pick up the rocks.

JONNY. Tell me you're sorry, Little Pig. Piggy.

> OSKAR *thinks. He looks at* MICKE. *And then back at* JONNY.

OSKAR. I'm sorry, Jonny.

JONNY. Do you believe him, Micke?

MICKE. No.

> OSKAR *turns and looks at* JONNY. *He is growing increasingly frightened at what they're going to do.*

OSKAR. I really am. I'm sorry.

JONNY. Lie down in the sand and tell me.

OSKAR. I'll ruin my clothes.

JONNY. And they'll cut their feet. Lie down in the sand and tell me you're sorry, bitch.

> OSKAR *lies in the sand.*

OSKAR. I'm sorry.

JONNY. Do you believe him, Micke?

> OSKAR *looks up to him, pleading.*

MICKE. No. I still don't believe him.

JONNY. Nor do I. Eat the sand. Eat the sand, Piggy. As God's penance. Eat the sand, bitch.

OSKAR. But little kids play in here. Piss in here.

> JONNY *raises his voice.*

JONNY. And you're lucky they're not bleeding in here. Eat the fucking sand, Piggy.

> OSKAR *eats the sand.*

MICKE. Now tell him you're sorry, bitch.

> OSKAR – *his mouth full of sand, a tear rolling down his face – looks up.*

OSKAR. I'm sorry.

JONNY. More sand.

OSKAR *eats more sand.* JONNY *laughs.*

OSKAR. I'm sorry. I'm sorry. I'm sorry. I'm sorry.

Scene Nine

ELI *is sitting on the jungle gym in the centre of the building.*
She looks more dishevelled than before.

OSKAR *approaches her.*

OSKAR. You again.

ELI. You again.

OSKAR. I came here to be by myself.

ELI. So did I.

OSKAR. Good. Then we should pretend we are alone.

OSKAR *sits and gets out his Rubik's Cube. He begins to
play with it.*

ELI *watches him.*

ELI. You've got sand on you.

OSKAR. I know.

ELI. Why?

OSKAR. I don't know why I should answer your questions.
We're not friends.

They slip back into silence. OSKAR *fiddles a new piece into
place on the Rubik's Cube.*

ELI. What's that?

OSKAR. For someone that wants to be alone, you're not very
good at being alone.

ELI. Yes, I am. I just want to know what that is…

OSKAR. Then you'll leave me alone?

ELI. If you'd like.

OSKAR. It's a Rubik's Cube.

ELI. What did you say?

OSKAR. Ru-bik's Cube.

ELI. And what is a Ru-bik's Cube?

> OSKAR *looks at her.*

> This is all part of the same question.

OSKAR. It's a puzzle.

ELI. A toy?

OSKAR. No. A puzzle.

ELI. How do they work?

OSKAR. You see the colours?

ELI. Naturally.

> OSKAR *laughs.*

OSKAR. 'Naturally.'

ELI. What?

OSKAR. 'Naturally'? You sound like an old person.

ELI. Do I?

OSKAR. Sometimes.

ELI. Come. Sit here. Tell me about the colours.

> OSKAR *looks at her.*

> I'm sorry if I upset you last time we spoke.

OSKAR. You didn't.

ELI. Then you should come and sit up here.

> OSKAR *climbs up to sit beside her.*

> Ru-bik's Cube.

OSKAR. You've got to turn it, and make the side all one colour.

ELI. You've made the side all white.

OSKAR. And the aim is to make all the sides a single colour.

ELI takes it out of his hand and studies it.

ELI. A good puzzle.

OSKAR. Yes.

ELI looks at OSKAR.

ELI. Do I still smell?

OSKAR sniffs.

OSKAR. Yes.

ELI. Smell bad?

OSKAR. Yes.

ELI. Smell like your wet dog?

OSKAR sniffs.

OSKAR. No. Now you smell like an infected bandage.

ELI. So not nice?

OSKAR. No. And your stomach makes funny noises.

ELI. I'm hungry.

OSKAR. Do you want some sweets?

ELI. No.

OSKAR. I don't mind.

ELI. No. Can I borrow this?

She indicates the Rubik's Cube.

OSKAR. Okay.

ELI. Thanks. I'll probably be here tomorrow.

OSKAR. Here?

ELI. And I'll try to smell better.

OSKAR. Okay.

ELI. Bye.

She dismounts – again with too much ease – and walks off and into the darkness. OSKAR *watches her go.*

OSKAR. Bye.

Scene Ten

OSKAR *is asleep in bed.*

A dark shadow approaches him.

MUM. Oskar? Oskar...

OSKAR. Mmm.

MUM. Oskar? Are you asleep...?

His MUM *comes into the light. She's drunk.*

OSKAR. Mmm?

MUM. Did you hear them?

OSKAR. Who?

MUM. Our new neighbours. You must have heard them. He was screaming and banging that door like he was crazy. And his daughter screamed back just as hard. Sometimes I'm so relieved I don't have a man at my back any more. Can I get in?

OSKAR. What?

MUM. Your bed. I'm cold.

OSKAR. Okay.

MUM. Blinds drawn all day. Probably alcoholics.

OSKAR. Mum?

MUM. Yes.

OSKAR. I want to sleep now.

MUM. Your dad called. Earlier. You were outside. I didn't tell you when you got back. I don't know why...

OSKAR. Okay. We'll talk about it in the morning.

MUM. Okay. Shall I stay here?

OSKAR. Okay.

> OSKAR *falls back asleep. His* MUM *listens.*

MUM. I can't hear them so badly in here.

> *She turns around and puts an arm around her son.*

You're a good boy, Oskar.

> OSKAR *is asleep. She looks at him a moment and then puts her head down herself.*

Scene Eleven

JOCKE *walks drunk down a street beside the woods.*

He sings a song to himself.

ELI. Please help me...

> JOCKE *stops. His eyes adjust to the darkness. He sees* ELI *lying crumpled under a street lamp.*

Help me... please.

> JOCKE *looks into the darkness.*

JOCKE. Who is that?

ELI. Help me, please.

> JOCKE *slowly approaches* ELI. *The sort of approach a drunk man makes. One foot finding its way followed by another foot.*

JOCKE. Were you... attacked?

ELI. Help me. Please. Lift me up.

JOCKE. Are you hurt? There is a murderer about…

ELI. Help me. Lift me up.

JOCKE. What happened to you?

ELI. Lift me up.

JOCKE. Is it your back? I shouldn't lift you if you've hurt your back.

ELI. Please.

JOCKE. I learnt that during military service.

ELI. Please, carry me.

JOCKE. Okay. I'll carry you to a place where we can call for help, right? Because it won't be safe leaving you while I went for help.

ELI. Please…

JOCKE kneels.

JOCKE. It's been a while since I lifted a woman, a girl, anyone really.

ELI. Okay.

JOCKE. Okay… So.

ELI. Thank you.

He gently lifts her. He's surprised at how easy it is.

JOCKE. Up we go. How does this feel?

ELI. Good.

JOCKE. Let's get you help.

ELI. Yes. I need so much help.

She sinks her teeth into his neck.

JOCKE. What…? That's my…

She starts to feed.

No. No. Fuck. Fuck. Fuck.

ELI *turns and twists in all directions, climbing up and over the man as she drinks his blood. It's beyond athletic. It's supernatural.*

He topples to the floor. She falls with him and, as he lands, continues to feed.

HAKAN *slowly approaches behind them. He watches the scene sadly.*

HAKAN. You've killed. You swore you wouldn't ever again.

ELI *turns towards him, her chin streaming with blood.*

ELI. And you swore you'd find me enough to eat. But you couldn't.

HAKAN. It isn't safe.

ELI. You'll make it safe. You'll dispose of the body.

HAKAN. I'll make it safe?

ELI. Yes. You're good at that.

HAKAN. You risked everything…

ELI. I was hungry.

HAKAN. You risked all we have.

ELI. We have nothing. I was hungry.

Pause.

HAKAN. Is this because of the boy?

ELI. Which boy?

HAKAN *is beginning to get angry.*

HAKAN. You think I haven't seen you? You think I haven't seen you?

ELI. You know I don't like it when you shout.

HAKAN. You deny me so much. Don't deny me the truth.

ELI. No. This is not because of the boy.

HAKAN. Because…

ELI. I told you – it's not because of the boy.

HAKAN *looks at her with pure love.*

HAKAN. I'm sorry you had to – I'm sorry I couldn't keep you fed.

ELI. You're getting older. Weaker. It's not your fault.

HAKAN. I try to love you as best I can.

ELI. I'm just not sure that's enough any more.

She turns back to eating.

Scene Twelve

OSKAR *sits alone on the jungle gym. He has a cut on his cheek. It's a new cut since last we saw him.*

He checks the time.

He moves his feet from side to side.

ELI. What happened to your face?

OSKAR *looks at* ELI.

OSKAR. You said you were going to be here yesterday.

ELI. Something happened.

OSKAR. All the same – you promised.

ELI. No. I didn't promise.

OSKAR *considers this.*

What happened to your face?

OSKAR. I… fell.

ELI. No. You didn't. Someone did that to you, didn't they?

OSKAR *thinks how to answer that question. He decides not to answer it.*

I finished your game.

OSKAR *looks at* ELI. *She holds up the Rubik's Cube.*

OSKAR *pulls himself to a stop.*

He walks over to ELI.

He takes the Rubik's Cube. He looks it up and down. It is complete.

OSKAR. Did you move the stickers?

ELI. No.

OSKAR. Do you promise?

ELI. I don't like promises...

OSKAR. Do you promise?

ELI. Yes. I promise. I didn't move the stickers. I turned the pieces. Do I smell better?

OSKAR. I don't know.

ELI. Smell me. Do I smell better?

OSKAR *smells.*

OSKAR. Yes. You smell better.

ELI. Smell me here.

She indicates under her chin. OSKAR *leans in and smells her under her chin.*

OSKAR. Yes. You smell better.

ELI *touches* OSKAR*'s wound, gently with just the tips of her fingers. Her face changes slightly as she does. She realises she's enjoying it and takes her fingers away.*

ELI. Someone did this, didn't they?

OSKAR. Yes.

ELI. Who?

OSKAR. Some friends.

ELI. You need to strike back. You've never done that, have you?

OSKAR. No.

ELI. So start now. Hit back. Hard.

OSKAR. There's two of them.

ELI. Then you have to hit harder. Use a weapon.

Stones, sticks. Hit them more than you really dare. Then they'll stop.

OSKAR. And if they keep hitting back?

ELI. You have a knife.

OSKAR. Yes, but what if they...

ELI. Then I'll help you.

OSKAR. You? But you are...

ELI. I can do it, Oskar. I promise I can help with that.

OSKAR looks at her carefully. He nods.

OSKAR. I've got you something.

ELI. Have you?

OSKAR climbs up the jungle gym and takes from his satchel the exercise book. He shows it her.

OSKAR. Our walls are next door to each other.

ELI. Yes.

OSKAR. This is Morse code.

ELI. Okay.

OSKAR. So we give information to each other, through the wall.

ELI. Is it a language?

OSKAR. Watch. This means dot.

He knuckles the wood.

This means dash.

He palms the wood.

Dot. Dash. Do you understand?

ELI. Yes.

OSKAR. My dad taught me this. I've made a copy for me too. Listen.

He knocks his knuckle on the wood. Then he pauses. Then he knocks his knuckle, followed by a palm, followed by a knuckle, then another knuckle, pause, then he does two more knuckles.

ELI. I don't understand.

OSKAR. Follow the code.

He repeats his phrase again.

What am I saying?

ELI *follows his hands. She smiles. And it's the first time we've really seen her properly smile.*

ELI. You're saying my name.

OSKAR. Yes. I'm saying your name.

Scene Thirteen

We're inside ELI's *flat. It's sparse.* HAKAN *is at the kitchen table.* ELI *comes in.*

HAKAN. Who were you with?

ELI. When?

HAKAN. I made clear I didn't want you to see him again.

ELI. He's there when I'm outside. Do you want me to stay inside all the time? Will that stop me seeing him… Will that make it better for you?

HAKAN. I made clear my feelings.

ELI. I know you did.

HAKAN *leaves the room.*

He returns with a flask of clear liquid.

What's that?

HAKAN. It's for when they catch me.

ELI. When?

HAKAN. They can't identify me. They've seen us together. If they identify me, they'll identify you.

ELI. So this will make you invisible?

HAKAN. As close as can be. It's sulphuric acid.

ELI realises what this means.

ELI. Oh.

HAKAN. I take this with me wherever I go. Whatever I do. I take it because it reminds me how much I love you.

ELI. Okay.

HAKAN. You don't even like me telling you I love you any more, do you?

ELI. You make it sound strange.

HAKAN. Will he do this for you?

ELI looks up at HAKAN.

ELI. I know how good you are to me. I'm grateful.

HAKAN looks at her carefully, studying her eyes.

HAKAN. Just not grateful enough.

Scene Fourteen

A school gym. There are pommel horses, mats, jump-ropes and chin-up bars.

MR AVILA *blows on a whistle and suddenly boys everywhere start moving around the stage. Amongst them,* OSKAR, MICKE *and* JONNY.

They jump the horse, land on the mats, do three skips on the ropes, pull themselves up on the chin-up bars twice and then start again. It's quite a sight. The only thing is, OSKAR *doesn't like the pommel horse, and when it gets to that apparatus he just runs around the side.*

MR AVILA. Faster. Harder. Better. Today you will do physical training and I will watch you. Monitor you. Micke, keep those sit-ups nice and tight.

OSKAR *runs around to the ropes. He's tripped by* JONNY. *He lands hard. He picks himself up, he keeps going.* JONNY *laughs.* MR AVILA *notices.*

No horseplay please, boys. If you are good then next week we will play ghost ball.

The boys all smile. Apart from OSKAR, *who grimaces. He is caught by* MR AVILA *as he goes around.*

Do the pommel.

OSKAR. I can't do it.

MR AVILA. Of course you can.

OSKAR. No. I can't.

MR AVILA. Imagine you really want something the other side. To help someone who you want to help, or to hurt someone you want to hurt.

OSKAR. That's silly.

MR AVILA. Do it to prove the other boys wrong.

OSKAR. That's silly too.

MR AVILA. Then jump because I tell you to.

OSKAR *thinks. He frowns at* MR AVILA. *Then he watches* JONNY *jump the pommel horse. He thinks and then runs and then jumps the pommel horse. He turns to his teacher with a smile.*

Good, Oskar, but next time try for more balance.

Scene Fifteen

HAKAN *stands in the bathroom. He splashes water on his face. There is a knocking from outside.*

He opens the door. ELI *walks into the bathroom and shuts the door. She is just in a robe. She looks at* HAKAN, *who looks back.*

ELI. Do you want me to take this off?

Pause.

Do you want me to take this off?

HAKAN. You're hungry. Are you hungry?

ELI. Yes.

HAKAN. I am sorry for disappointing you.

ELI. Do you want me to take this off?

HAKAN. I want you to love me.

ELI. Well this is as close as I can get.

HAKAN. I'm sorry for not being what you need. I think now I'm getting stronger –

ELI. Tonight we will lie together.

HAKAN. We will?

ELI. We will.

HAKAN. I can lie next to you? Hold you?

ELI. Yes.

HAKAN. For the whole night?

ELI. Yes.

HAKAN. But please… You should… Keep your clothes on.

ELI *nods*.

ELI. Okay.

HAKAN. Thank you.

He looks at her a moment more.

For the whole night?

ELI. Yes.

HAKAN. Thank you.

Scene Sixteen

MR AVILA *is putting away the apparatus. He doesn't notice* OSKAR *watching him until he pushes the pommel horse offstage and uncovers* OSKAR *sitting behind it.*

MR AVILA. Oskar. Reliving your triumph?

OSKAR. Yes. I think so.

MR AVILA *smiles at* OSKAR*'s forthright response.*

The training sessions you run on Thursdays?

MR AVILA. The strength-training classes?

OSKAR. Yes. Do I have to sign up or…

MR AVILA. No need to sign up. Just come. Thursdays at seven o'clock. At the swimming pool. You want to do it?

OSKAR. Yes, I… Yes.

MR AVILA. That is good. You train. Then you can do the pull-up bar… fifty times…

MR AVILA *mimes doing the pull-up bar.*

OSKAR. No. I won't be able to do that, but yes, I'll be there.

MR AVILA. Then I see you Thursday. Good.

OSKAR walks away. MR AVILA watches him go.

Scene Seventeen

ELI is lying with HAKAN sleeping beside her.

There is the sound of knocking through the wall.

ELI listens intently.

'G–O–I–N–G O–U–T.' is signalled.

ELI smiles. She looks at HAKAN. He stirs. She is more hesitant.

'I–M C–O–M–I–N–G.' she knocks.

Then she stands in her robe, and walks out of the room.
HAKAN stirs again. But doesn't wake.

Scene Eighteen

The sweet shop. OSKAR and ELI carefully walk between the rows. They are playing some sort of game with each other. It involves mostly stealing. KURT watches on, slightly confused.

OSKAR. You know, they call this the lovers' kiosk?

ELI. They do, why?

She slips a chocolate bar into OSKAR's pocket, he smiles.

OSKAR. The guy who owns it…

ELI. That guy?

OSKAR. He invites women back here, after closing. I heard them say so at school. I heard the teachers say so.

ELI. He invites them back here? To eat all the sweets?

OSKAR. I'm guessing so.

ELI. And then makes love to them?

OSKAR. I'm guessing so.

ELI. But he looks like a monkey.

   OSKAR *laughs,* KURT *looks up.*

KURT. I remember you.

OSKAR. Yes.

KURT. Is this your friend?

ELI. Yes. This is his friend. And she would like a banaaaana.

KURT. A banana?

ELI. Yes. Do you stock banannanas?

   OSKAR *is trying really hard to suppress a giggle.*

KURT. No. We only stock sweets. We have foam bananas.

ELI. Then we will have foam bananas instead.

   KURT *frowns.*

KURT. Okay.

   ELI *scoops all the foam bananas into a bag.*

ELI. We want all your foam bananas. And we've no time for
   monkeying around.

KURT. Okay. They'll be expensive.

ELI. I don't intend on paying you in peanuts, my man. Hang the
   expense. We've no time for aping about.

   OSKAR *can't help a peal of laughter emerge from him.*

   ELI *lays down some serious notes on the table and then they
   run out of the shop.*

Scene Nineteen

They run and run and run and finally slump down in peals of laughter.

OSKAR *eats some of the bananas. And then offers the bag to* ELI.

She shakes her head.

ELI. I can't.

OSKAR. You can't what?

ELI. I can't eat sweets.

OSKAR. You can't eat sweets. But you bought the shop!

ELI. No. I didn't buy the shop. Just all the foam bananas.

OSKAR. You don't know what you're missing. These are good.

ELI. I don't. You're right. I don't even know what they taste like. Sweets.

OSKAR. You haven't even tasted one? A sweet? Ever?

ELI. No.

OSKAR. Then how do you know you can't…

ELI. I just know. That's all.

Pause.

OSKAR. You're rich.

ELI. I am.

OSKAR. Is your dad really important?

ELI. I don't think so.

OSKAR. Then how come you are rich?

ELI. I just am.

OSKAR. We sometimes hear you and your dad arguing through the wall.

ELI. Do you?

OSKAR. Yes.

   OSKAR *suddenly leans in and hugs her. They stay in the hug.*
   They stay in the hug for ages.

   Is this okay?

ELI. Yes.

OSKAR. Is this nice?

   ELI *thinks.*

ELI. Yes.

OSKAR. Okay.

ELI. Okay.

   They dislocate from the hug.

OSKAR. Okay.

   They stand a moment more.

   It was nice for me too.

ELI. Oskar, do you like me?

OSKAR. Yes.

   Beat.

   Yes. I think I like you a lot.

ELI. Would you still like me if I turned out to not be a girl?

   OSKAR *freezes.*

OSKAR. What do you mean?

ELI. Just that. Would you still like me if I turned out to not be
   a girl?

   OSKAR *thinks with a frown.*

OSKAR. Yes… I guess so.

ELI. Are you sure?

OSKAR. Why do you ask?

ELI. I just wanted to know. Shall we hug again?

OSKAR. We could.

ELI. But we don't need to.

OSKAR. No.

ELI. I will take that sweet.

OSKAR. Yes?

> *He holds at the bag, she takes a banana from him. She eats it. He frowns at her.*

> Nice?

ELI. Very nice. Bye, Oskar.

OSKAR. Bye, Eli.

> *He thinks and then walks away.*

> *She watches him go.*

> *And then she vomits up the sweet.*

> *She wipes her face and then walks off after him.*

Scene Twenty

OSKAR *sits in a locker room. Other boys get changed – unashamed of their bodies – around him. Amongst them is* JONNY *and* MICKE. *There's various banter, we don't pick it out.*

OSKAR *covers himself with a towel.*

JONNY. Nice pecs, Piggy.

> OSKAR *covers his chest.*

> You giving us a striptease? Are you going to show us your hairy balls?

MICKE. He hasn't got hairy balls.

JONNY. I know that, he knows that.

OSKAR *says nothing.*

Do you want to see my hairy balls, Piggy?

MICKE. Come on, we'll be late, Avila will make us do lengths.

JONNY. We want to do lengths, we come here to do lengths, you want to see my hairy balls, Piggy?

JONNY *looks around – by now most of the boys have changed and left the changing room for the session.*

MICKE. Come on, Jonny.

JONNY *thinks and then turns his towel into a whip and whips OSKAR with it. Then he exits. He's the last to leave – other than OSKAR.*

Who is left alone.

He takes a breath. And then he takes off his trousers.

OSKAR *takes out his swimming costume.*

And then he sits again and puts a towel over himself. Behind him – through a high-up window – soundlessly slips HAKAN. He falls to the floor – uncomfortably but silently. The window closes behind him.

HAKAN *carries his gas canister with him and his funnel. He looks at OSKAR and then carefully approaches him.*

OSKAR *carefully takes off his pants under the towel – and starts to ease his swimming shorts on. And his swimming shorts get slightly stuck.*

And then MR AVILA comes into view and HAKAN drops from view despairingly.

MR AVILA. Oskar, you coming?

OSKAR *looks at MR AVILA slightly hopelessly. MR AVILA smiles at him kindly.*

You're the only one in here. Your body is nothing to be ashamed of.

OSKAR. They don't think so.

MR AVILA. Oskar, whatever they say just ignore…

OSKAR. Mr Avila, how do you know when you're in love?

MR AVILA. Oh, I… that is a large question…

He thinks. He sits beside OSKAR.

It depends on who you are, but… I would say that it's when you know… or at least when you really believe that this is the person you always want to be with.

OSKAR. You mean, when you feel you can't live without that person.

MR AVILA *smiles.*

MR AVILA. I think that might be a grand way of putting it, but okay.

OSKAR. And if I wasn't in love – with a girl?

MR AVILA *looks at* OSKAR.

MR AVILA. Two men, can also love each other, it's not my personal choice, but it's possible.

OSKAR. Okay.

MR AVILA *isn't sure what to say next.*

MR AVILA. It gets easier. As you get older, it gets easier. I promise you that, Oskar. All this gets easier.

OSKAR *nods.*

Now, I have some strength-testing to do, will you come join the class?

OSKAR *nods. He pulls his swimming costume up. He exits after* MR AVILA.

And HAKAN *stands. He thinks.*

He returns to the window. He looks up. It's too high. He looks at the door MR AVILA *and* OSKAR *have left by. He hasn't thought this through.*

And then MICKE *re-enters the locker room – he's in swimming trunks and wet.* HAKAN *stays frozen in place.*

MICKE *takes his goggles from inside his locker and then looks to exit back out when he notices* HAKAN.

MICKE. Who are you?

HAKAN *turns and looks at* MICKE.

This pool is for kids. You one of those perverts?

HAKAN *looks at him sadly, and then twists* MICKE, *holding his gas mask to* MICKE*'s face.* MICKE *sinks to the floor.*

HAKAN *moves quickly. He picks up a towel and winds it around the door handle, tying it closed.*

He then fits the gas mask over the boy's head.

He fits some rope around the clothes hangers. He begins to pull the boy so that he's hanging upside down.

There is some knocking at the door. HAKAN *looks towards it despairingly.*

There is some more knocking.

MR AVILA (*off*). What's going on in there? This door isn't supposed to be locked. Ever.

HAKAN *gets his knife out. He puts it on* MICKE*'s throat.*

There is more knocking. And then a bang.

Open this door, do you hear me? Open this door.

HAKAN *smoothes* MICKE*'s hair back. He thinks. He realises he's not going to kill again. He puts the knife down.*

There is another bang. Then another bang... The door splinters. They're going to get the door open.

HAKAN *calmly takes the sulphuric acid out of his bag.*

Bang. Bang. Bang. The door is coming off.

HAKAN. Eli.

He pours acid all over his face.

He screams as it burns him.

HAKAN *screams and screams and screams.*

The door is bust down.

MR AVILA *looks horrified at the scene he finds.*

Scene Twenty-One

OSKAR *sits in a police holding room. His* MUM *is in a fierce fight with* HALMBERG.

MUM. I'm complaining because I want to take my son home…

HALMBERG. And we want you to take him home – but he was the last person in that room and…

MUM. My son just underwent great trauma.

HALMBERG. You do understand that I'm trying to run a murder investigation here…

MUM. I do understand, do you understand I want what's best for my son?

HALMBERG. Have you been drinking?

MUM. Is that business of yours?

HALMBERG. I will keep your son as long as I need to keep your son, do you understand, ma'am?

MUM. Who do I complain to?

HALMBERG. Whoever you fucking like…

Scene Twenty-Two

OSKAR *is sitting in bed.*

Suddenly there is a knock at the window.

ELI *is outside it. Obscured by a curtain.*

ELI. Oskar?

She knocks again.

Can I come in? Say that I can come in?

OSKAR. Wait a moment.

He makes to get out of bed.

ELI. No. Stay in bed. Just say that I can come in.

OSKAR. You can come in.

ELI. Close your eyes.

OSKAR *closes his eyes.*

The window opens. Snow blows in.

Then ELI climbs in. She's naked. She gets into his bed.

Don't turn around.

OSKAR. Okay.

Pause.

Are you naked?

ELI. Yes. Is that disgusting?

OSKAR. No. But aren't you freezing?

ELI. No.

OSKAR. Shall we play a game?

ELI. What game would you like?

OSKAR. Slithering snakes running down your back, which one did that.

He holds up his fingers.

She doesn't know to turn and look at his fingers. He frowns.

You're supposed to tell me which finger did that? Touched your back last.

ELI *thinks. She doesn't turn around.*

ELI. Your middle finger of your left hand.

OSKAR *is surprised.*

OSKAR. How did you know that?

ELI. I don't know. It's the finger with the longest nail. I notice things.

OSKAR *studies his finger. He looks at his hands generally. And then he looks at* ELI. *He gently touches her hair. She smiles.*

OSKAR. I saw some things I didn't want to see tonight. All that I thought – when I was seeing them – was I wish you were there.

ELI. Yes?

OSKAR. Eli, will you go out with me?

ELI. What does that mean?

OSKAR. I don't mind if you're a boy.

ELI. I'm not a boy.

OSKAR *frowns – confused.*

OSKAR. But – you said you weren't a girl…

ELI. I'm nothing. Not a child. Not old. Not a boy. Not a girl. Nothing.

OSKAR. Okay.

ELI. I'm just me.

OSKAR. Okay.

He frowns.

So will you go out with me or not?

ELI. Oskar, I'd like to but… can't we just be together like we already are?

OSKAR *shrivels up slightly. He turns over away from her.*

OSKAR. Okay.

ELI. Are you sad? We can kiss, if you like…

OSKAR. I don't want to kiss.

    ELI *turns over towards him, looks at his back.*

ELI. Do you do – anything in particular with someone you're going out with?

OSKAR. No.

    ELI *thinks and then smiles.*

ELI. Then we can go out.

    OSKAR *turns over, they face each other.*

OSKAR. We can?

ELI. Yes.

OSKAR. Good.

    They lie together.

    Eli?

ELI. Mm?

OSKAR. I'm glad you came over.

ELI. Me too.

    Pause.

    Oskar?

OSKAR. Mmm?

ELI. Do I smell tonight?

OSKAR. I don't mind it. You smell like you.

    ELI *considers this and then itches her nose and then smiles.*

ELI. Okay.

    Lights slowly fade.

    Interval.

ACT TWO

Scene One

Hospital reception. ELI *walks in. Her hair is wet, she looks around disconcertingly.* NILS *is the hospital receptionist.*

ELI. Excuse me…

NILS. Can I help you?

ELI. I'm looking for my father…

NILS. I see, has he been admitted here?

ELI. Yes. I think so. Although I don't know for sure?

NILS. Should you be all alone here? At this hour?

ELI. I just wanted to know if he is here.

NILS. Then let's see if I can help. What's his name?

ELI. I don't know.

    NILS *frowns.*

NILS. You don't know?

ELI. No.

NILS. But he is your father – you must know his name…

ELI. He uses different names. The police took him.

NILS. The police?

ELI. They're keeping him here. Because he's sick.

    NILS *scratches his face.*

NILS. Well, what kind of illness does he have?

ELI. I don't know.

NILS. Maybe you should talk to the police. Shall I fetch someone down…?

ELI. I just wanted to know which window was his, so I could... know.

NILS *is now thoroughly confused.*

NILS. He'll be on the top floor. I'm sure we can arrange a way – I'll fetch someone down.

ELI. No. Don't. No, I know enough now...

ELI *walks away.* NILS *notices she's not wearing any shoes.*

NILS. But you're not wearing any shoes.

ELI *speeds up.*

And it's snowing.

He exits after ELI. *He looks out into the cold snowing night. He can't see* ELI *anywhere.*

Scene Two

HALMBERG *sits beside* HAKAN's *bed.* HAKAN *is horribly disfigured.*

HALMBERG. I understand that you won't speak. But perhaps you can nod if you hear what I'm saying? Can you nod?

Behind HALMBERG *we see* ELI *begin to climb the wall.*

No? No. You had a paper with some Morse code on it. What meaning does that have? Were you using it? Will you use it now to talk to me? One tap for yes, two taps for no.

Are you involved in some kind of cult?

ELI *climbs up and over everything.*

We would like to know who you are, you see...

HAKAN *says nothing.*

We'll find that out, sooner or later. You could save us some legwork by communicating with us now.

HALMBERG *leans in and whispers.* ELI *climbs up and up, she's relentless. And brilliant.*

We will find out everything about you. We will ruin you. No one does that to people. No one does.

ELI *reaches* HAKAN*'s window and sits in the window pane.* HAKAN *notices her and smiles.* ELI *doesn't smile.*

HALMBERG *notices* HAKAN*'s smile but not where it is headed.*

Fuck you. You know that? Fuck you.

He walks out of the room.

And ELI *looks at* HAKAN. *He looks back… He indicates 'come in'.*

She climbs in through the window.

ELI. Hello.

Pause. ELI *walks over to him. She touches his face. He winces in pain – but doesn't try to stop her – touches her hands.*

Were you after him? Were you there after him? Were you going to feed me his blood?

HAKAN *says nothing.* ELI *breaks into a sort of tears.*

You were, weren't you? Why would you do that?

HAKAN *looks at her. When he speaks it is with a husk that sounds inhuman.*

HAKAN. You… are… so… beautiful.

ELI *cries deeply now, she curls up beside* HAKAN *on the bed, she curls into him.* HAKAN *smiles.*

Before… I put it on… my face. I thought about… the time we had… together. I thought about you as… an… angel, coming down… from Heaven, spreading your… wings, and carrying me off to a place we could be together. For ever.

ELI *says nothing.*

HAKAN *raises his neck towards her.*

Forgive me, Eli.

ELI *looks at him, she thinks. And then she bites into his neck, she begins to feed from him.*

And then she breaks off.

ELI. I can taste morphine.

He looks at her. She looks back. A tear rolls down his acid-scarred face.

She kisses his head. She breaks his neck.

Scene Three

OSKAR *is standing on top of the jungle gym as* ELI *approaches him.*

OSKAR. I've decided I'm not interested in violence. Now that they've caught the killer. I've decided I've no need for violence.

ELI. You're holding a knife.

OSKAR. No. I'm holding a sword.

ELI. It looks like a knife.

OSKAR. It's a sword. I've decided I'm a knight.

ELI. Don't knights like violence?

OSKAR. And you as my – girlfriend... Is girlfriend okay?

ELI. Girlfriend is okay.

OSKAR. Must be the beautiful – maiden – is maiden okay?

ELI. I can be a princess even.

OSKAR. Because you as my princess... I need to rescue you from the dragon basically.

ELI. You are silly.

OSKAR. No, I'm just happy.

ELI. This is happy?

OSKAR. I used to make up stories all the time when I was a kid.

ELI. You're still a kid.

OSKAR. No. I'm not.

> ELI *looks at him.*

> You look sad.

ELI. What if I'm the dragon?

OSKAR. You can be the dragon. I don't want to fight you then.
But you could be the dragon.

ELI. You'd rather I was the princess?

OSKAR. Yes.

ELI. Okay. I'll be the princess.

> *She pulls herself up onto the jungle gym. She lies across the
> top of it.* OSKAR *balances across beside her.*

OSKAR. Eli, do you want to do something?

ELI. We can do something.

OSKAR. Now that we're in love.

ELI. Are we in love?

OSKAR. Now that we're going out.

ELI. We are going out.

OSKAR. Now that we've slept together.

> ELI *sits up on her elbows and smiles.*

ELI. That isn't what people mean when they say slept together.

OSKAR. I know that. I do go to school. I was just – enjoying –
our – history.

ELI. Okay. We've slept together.

OSKAR. Do you want to enter a pact with me?

ELI. I will enter any pact you choose, brave knight.

OSKAR nods. And then puts his knife inside his hand. He pulls his fist tight around it. And then pulls the blade through.

OSKAR. Ow. Ow.

She sees what he's done. She looks at him. Her face goes white.

ELI. What did you just do?

OSKAR. It's easy, Eli, it wasn't even...

ELI looks at the blood – she begins to transform.

ELI. What did you do?

OSKAR. It will be a bond. Like in books. A bond. We'll be sealed by blood. You've got to do it. You promised.

ELI. I hate promises.

OSKAR. It almost doesn't hurt at all. You don't have to do as much as I did. Just prick yourself in the finger or something. Then we'll mix our blood.

ELI. Oskar... we can't... why did you do this?

A drop of blood falls from his hand onto the floor. ELI kneels in front of it, bends her head to it, licks it up.

OSKAR. What did you just do?

ELI. Leave.

OSKAR begins to cry.

OSKAR. Eli, stop it. Stop playing.

ELI. Go. Or you'll die.

OSKAR. Eli...

ELI looks up fully transformed. Her voice deepened.

ELI. Go. Go. Get out of here.

OSKAR *runs. He runs like there's no tomorrow. He gets away as fast as possible.*

ELI *stays on all fours. Licking at the blood he's left.*

Then she throws her head back and screams.

Scene Four

A frozen lake.

OSKAR *is ice-skating with his class.*

Kids are screaming and dancing and having a good time. OSKAR *isn't.*

MR AVILA *is in charge. He has a whistle he blows every now and again when he sees something he doesn't like.*

JONNY. Having fun, Piggy?

MICKE. He is smiling.

JONNY. Is Piggy having fun? What's he thinking about?

OSKAR. Nothing.

JONNY. Lot of water round here.

MICKE. Ice.

 JONNY *turns to* MICKE, *irritated.*

JONNY. Ice is water. Prick.

MICKE. Yes.

JONNY. And you know what water says to me, Micke?

MICKE. No.

JONNY. A bath.

MICKE. A bath?

JONNY. Did the acid man take your brain cells as well as your virginity? Yes. A bath. And you know who needs a bath?

MICKE. No.

JONNY. It's obvious, Micke. Piggy needs a bath. It's in his name.

OSKAR. No.

JONNY. Piggy smells like shit and needs to wash.

He grabs OSKAR *by the arms.*

OSKAR. No.

JONNY. Help me.

MICKE *grabs* OSKAR *too.*

MICKE. Don't struggle, Piggy.

OSKAR. Micke...

JONNY. He said don't struggle. We're only doing what's best for you, bitch. And sir's too busy looking at the girls with their hard nipples.

OSKAR. Let me go.

JONNY. Piggy smells like shit and needs to wash. Where's the ice broken, Micke?

MICKE. Over – here.

OSKAR. No. It'll be cold.

JONNY. Break the ice more, Micke. He'll want to get in deep.

OSKAR. Help. HELP.

JONNY. Scream away, bitch. They can't hear you.

OSKAR *gets away – wriggling out of* JONNY*'s grasp – and grabs whatever he can. He grabs a stick.*

He turns and swings it, it hits JONNY*'s shin.*

Fuck. Ow. That hurts, Piggy. You just hurt me, Piggy.

OSKAR *swings again, this time* JONNY *slides out of the way.*

Put that down, bitch, or I'll break you. Get it?

OSKAR *swings a third time, higher this time,* JONNY *ducks, the stick makes hard contact with the outside of* JONNY*'s head.*

JONNY *falls to the ice, bleeding.*

MICKE. Shit.

JONNY *begins to fit on the ice.*

Sir. Sir. Sir.

MR AVILA *begins to run over towards them. He blows his whistle.*

OSKAR. I didn't mean to hurt him.

MICKE. Sir.

JONNY *curls into a fetal position. He whimpers.*

OSKAR *just stands looking utterly ill.*

OSKAR. I didn't mean… I didn't mean…

And then he drops the stick.

MR AVILA. What the hell has happened here?

OSKAR *looks at* MR AVILA.

OSKAR. You could have helped me with them. You could have helped.

Scene Five

OSKAR *sits on the stairs. His* MUM *is on the phone.*

MUM. They're going to call me and ask me what I've done wrong...

Oh yes, they will, and what do I say? Sorry, but you see, my boy doesn't have a father and that...

Then live up to it then...

No, you haven't...

I think you should talk to him then...

I think you should talk to him...

She gestures the phone to OSKAR.

Your father wants to talk to you.

OSKAR *takes the receiver carefully.*

OSKAR. Hello?...

Yes...

Yes...

But I didn't mean to...

I was trying to hit his shoulder...

I didn't mean to...

Will he be okay?...

His face begins to contort, he begins to cry.

Do you think he'll be okay?

MUM. Your dad doesn't know that, does he? I talked to the school, not him.

OSKAR. I didn't mean it...

I didn't mean any of it...

MUM. You've let us all down.

MUM *takes the phone from* OSKAR.

He will be with you soon.

She puts the phone down.

OSKAR. You never ask the right questions. You never say the right things.

MUM. And that's why you're going to your father's, okay? That's why you're going to your father's...

OSKAR. And you're drunk – again.

His MUM *slaps him.*

MUM. You think I shouldn't drink? Look at you. A savage! A hooligan! I produce this and I shouldn't drink.

OSKAR *bolts out of the room.*

Oskar... Oskar, I didn't mean it... Oskar!

Scene Six

OSKAR *and his* DAD *sit, a draughtboard laid out in front of them.* OSKAR's DAD *makes a move and then looks up and smiles at his son.*

DAD. The snow is a little loose for the skis. When it gets better we'll go out there and get some pretty good speed up.

OSKAR. Yes? We should do that.

DAD. Yes. That's what I was thinking.

OSKAR. Great.

Pause. OSKAR's DAD *makes a move.* OSKAR *immediately makes a follow-up. His* DAD *looks at the board, frowns, and then rubs his face.*

I like this place. It's never changed.

DAD. Great. How's your mother?

OSKAR. Much the same.

DAD. She probably tries her best.

His DAD *finally makes a move.* OSKAR *retaliates. His* DAD *makes a move.* OSKAR *smiles and makes another. His* DAD *frowns.*

Are you going to beat me again!

OSKAR. Dad, do you think you have a – do you think you grow into a certain type of person – can you tell what – type of person I'm going to grow into?

DAD. What sort of adult?

OSKAR. Yes.

His DAD *looks at the board. He smiles.*

DAD. Yes, I think you're going to be the sort of person that beats me at games.

OSKAR. I've got a friend I've been practising with. She's really good.

DAD. Is she now? Have you got a girlfriend, Oskar?

OSKAR *says nothing.*

I had my first girlfriend about your age. She was called Astrid.

OSKAR. Did you love her?

DAD. I thought I did.

OSKAR. Where is she now?

DAD. I have no idea.

OSKAR *looks up at his* DAD *with a frown.*

OSKAR. I don't think she's my girlfriend any more.

His DAD *smiles.*

DAD. She's left you?

OSKAR. I think I would like to stay here –

DAD. Stay here?

OSKAR. For as long as you will have me…

His DAD *blushes.*

DAD. Oskar, that's a complicated area…

OSKAR. We can make it simple.

DAD. No. We can't.

OSKAR. Dad…

DAD. The answer is no. Now, let's just get on with the game…

Suddenly there is a knocking at the door. His DAD *rises.*
OSKAR *frowns at the door.*

OSKAR. Don't answer it, Dad.

DAD. Why shouldn't I answer it?

He answers the door. JANNE *enters.*

Janne!

You remember my boy?

JANNE. Of course I do… Hi, Oskar, you've got big, how's it
going?

OSKAR *sits up and away from the food.*

OSKAR. Fine.

JANNE. I see you're playing draughts.

DAD. Yes, but the boy is too good for me. I can't beat him any
more. He's been practising. With a girl. With an ex-girlfriend.

JANNE. Never trust girls when it comes to games of skill. They
have more skill than we can hope for. It's why we have to be
stronger than them. Do you dare play against me then, Oskar?

OSKAR *shakes his head.*

OSKAR. No.

DAD. Don't be rude, Oskar.

OSKAR. I'm not being rude. I don't want to play with him. We
were playing.

DAD. And now we've got a guest…

JANNE. I'm interrupting.

DAD. Of course you're not.

>DAD *exits to the pantry.* JANNE *looks at* OSKAR *coolly.*

JANNE. Anyone ever tell you, you need a haircut?

OSKAR. No.

JANNE. How long are you here for?

>OSKAR*'s* DAD *re-enters with a bottle of homemade vodka and two glasses.*

>Well, well, what have we here…

DAD. Just a little something I made earlier.

>JANNE *laughs.* OSKAR *stands and walks from the room.*

JANNE. Where's he going now?

DAD. Ignore him. He's been playing up.

OSKAR. I'll go home in the morning.

DAD. Your mother's right. You've become impossible.

OSKAR. Then better you don't have to worry about me.

DAD. Yes, okay.

>*He opens the vodka. He pours a glass for him and* JANNE.

>OSKAR *exits in disgust.*

>It's so hard when you don't get the chance to discipline them.

JANNE. We'll be okay.

DAD. I'll drink to that.

Scene Seven

OSKAR *sits in his kitchen.*

There is a knocking at his door.

ELI (*outside*). I know you're in there, Oskar. I know you're back.

Pause.

And I know your mother isn't there. I saw her leave.

Pause.

Please, Oskar. I just want to explain.

OSKAR *walks over and opens the door, it swings open wide. The two look at each other.*

It's good to see you again.

Beat.

Is it good to see me?

OSKAR. That's something only old people ask.

Beat.

ELI. Where have you been? Why didn't you tell me where you were going?

OSKAR. What are you?

ELI. What do you think I am?

OSKAR. I don't know.

ELI. I'm not that. I live on blood. But I am not... that... Can I come in?

OSKAR. What's the difference?

ELI. I choose not to be that. So I'm not – that.

OSKAR. Are you... dead?

ELI *smiles.*

ELI. No. Can't you tell?

OSKAR. No, but I mean... did you die once, a long time ago?

ELI. I've lived for a long time.

OSKAR. Do you want to kill me?

ELI. If I'd have wanted to do that – wouldn't I have done it already…

OSKAR. But you drank my blood.

ELI. Only because it was there.

OSKAR. Are there a lot of you? This – thing that you are?

ELI. I'm not a thing.

OSKAR. Then what are you?

ELI. Eli.

OSKAR. But that's your name.

ELI. Yes.

OSKAR. What's your full name?

ELI. My name used to be Elias Jannson. My name now is Eli.

OSKAR. But Elias is a boy's name.

ELI. Yes.

OSKAR. I don't understand.

ELI. If you invite me in it will be easier.

OSKAR. But maybe I shouldn't invite you in, Elias.

ELI. Are you angry because my name is Elias?

OSKAR *raises his voice.*

OSKAR. No! I told you I wanted to go out with you even if you were a boy!

ELI. Are you going to invite me in or not, Oskar?

OSKAR. What happens if I don't?

ELI *thinks and steels her jaw bravely.*

She steps into the room. She shuts the door behind her. Nothing happens. There's a long pause.

Is that all?

ELI. Wait.

Suddenly a tear falls out of the corner of her eye, a tear of blood.

Then ELI *starts to flush, she flushes wine-red, and her hands tighten into fists as pores in her face open and tiny pearls of blood appear in dots all over her skin. And then her throat, and then the rest of her body.*

Her lips twist in pain, and drops of blood run out of the corners of her mouth. Her eyes now flow with blood, and her clothes are becoming soaked with it. She's bleeding out of all the pores in her body. OSKAR *watches all this with mounting horror.*

OSKAR. No... No... I didn't mean... You can come in... you can... you are welcome, you are... allowed to be here...

ELI's face relaxes. Her clench fists loosen. The grimace of pain disappears. She stands for a moment.

Have I said enough? Will it stop now?

She opens her eyes, her eyes are back to normal, but the rest of her is covered with blood. She is drenched in blood.

Sorry... I... didn't think... I didn't know... Have I said enough? Has it stopped?

ELI. Yes. It's stopped.

OSKAR. I'm so sorry.

ELI. Don't be.

OSKAR. I'm so sorry.

ELI. I'm not.

OSKAR. I never want to hurt you – I never will hurt you.

ELI. I know you won't.

Pause.

I think I've ruined your carpet.

OSKAR. That's okay, we'll say the dog did it.

ELI. Your dog is dead.

OSKAR. Oh yeah.

Scene Eight

HALMBERG *is presenting to his colleagues. He looks somehow broken. He hasn't slept in a long time.*

HALMBERG. Thank you for coming.

As many of you know we found another body last night. Our fifth. I'm still interested in pursuing the fact that Hakan Kolmstun was working with a partner. But there are those who want to stretch the investigation – wider. Those who think we got the wrong man.

They'll be sending someone from the city today who'll be taking on many of my responsibilities.

I want to tell you how grateful I am for all the support you've given me and to tell you that my door is always open. For any of you.

And that is all I have to say.

Scene Nine

OSKAR*'s* MUM *stands with a desperate smile on her face. The clock ticks extra loudly in the background.*

MUM. I made your favourite.

OSKAR. Thank you.

Pause.

MUM. Call it a welcome home…

OSKAR. Thank you.

Pause. They lapse back into silence.

MUM. The carpet has a stain on it, did you notice?

OSKAR. I vomited. Will it clean away?

MUM. Probably.

Beat.

OSKAR. Mum, where did you and Dad meet?

MUM. That's a funny question. In a bar, I think.

OSKAR. Where did you first kiss?

MUM (*laughs*). In the same bar.

OSKAR. When did you realise it wasn't going to work?

Beat. She frowns at her son.

MUM. I don't know, Oskar.

Pause.

OSKAR. I've decided I'm going to write a note to Jonny.
Saying sorry about his ear.

MUM. That sounds good.

OSKAR nods.

Your dad phoned. Told me what you said. It's up to you,
Oskar. Where you live. Which of us you live with.

OSKAR. Maybe I'll live with neither of you.

MUM. That's not possible. It's not. Now come and eat your food.

OSKAR. I'm not sure it's my favourite any more.

MUM. Eat it anyway.

Scene Ten

ELI *puts on a record. It's 'La Mer' sung by Charles Trenet.*

OSKAR *stands in her apartment. It's a drab apartment. It's even more bare than last time we saw it.*

ELI. You like this music?

OSKAR. Yes. What does it mean?

ELI. It's saying nice things.

OSKAR. That old man who was here before. That wasn't your dad, was it?

ELI. No.

OSKAR. Was he also a… someone who – needs blood?

ELI. No.

OSKAR. And have you… how long have you been together?

ELI. A while.

Beat. OSKAR *looks around.*

OSKAR. I thought you were rich.

ELI. I am rich.

OSKAR. Then why does this place look so – poor.

ELI *thinks and then walks over to and takes a jewelled egg out of the trunk. She gives it to* OSKAR.

ELI. What's it worth, do you think?

OSKAR. I don't know. What is it?

ELI. There are only two of them in the whole world. If you sold one you could buy yourself… a nuclear power plant, maybe.

OSKAR. Yes?

ELI. Well, I don't know, what does a nuclear power plant cost? Fifty million?

OSKAR. I think it would cost… billions…

ELI *laughs.*

ELI. Oh, in that case, you probably couldn't...

OSKAR. What would you do with a nuclear power plant anyway?

ELI. Open it.

> OSKAR *does exactly that and light shines from within the egg. It's spectacular.*

OSKAR. Wow.

ELI. Yes.

OSKAR. It's beautiful.

ELI. Yes.

OSKAR. What's it for?

ELI. I don't know. Having.

> ELI *takes it from him.*

Do you want money?

OSKAR. No. Did you steal it – that?

ELI. No. It was given me.

OSKAR. Okay.

ELI. Will you dance with me, Oskar?

OSKAR. I hurt someone.

ELI. Did you? Someone that had hurt you?

OSKAR. Yes.

ELI. And you felt bad about it?

OSKAR. Very.

ELI. Then that probably makes you better than me. Will you dance with me, Oskar?

OSKAR. Okay.

> *He approaches her. She puts her arms around him. They begin to dance.*

ELI. What are you thinking?

OSKAR. That I feel – safe.

ELI. Are we still in love, Oskar?

OSKAR. Probably.

ELI. Good.

Beat. She lifts her head. They softly kiss on the lips.

Are you going to go home?

OSKAR. Not tonight.

ELI. Soon I will have to sleep.

OSKAR. Yes?

ELI. The sun is coming up.

OSKAR. Yes. Where will you sleep?

ELI. In here.

She indicates the trunk.

OSKAR. In there?

ELI. It's quite nice. I've made it comfortable.

OSKAR. Okay.

She looks at the trunk and then up at OSKAR.

ELI. I'm not sure I'm very good for you, Oskar.

OSKAR. I'm not sure either.

ELI. Shall we kiss again?

OSKAR. Okay.

ELI kisses OSKAR. Lights slowly fade.

Scene Eleven

OSKAR *is asleep beside the trunk.*

There is a knock at the door.

There is another knock at the door.

HALMBERG (*outside*). Hello?

There is another knock. OSKAR *wakes up.*

Hello. My name is Police Commissioner Halmberg. I have reason to believe this is the former residence of Hakan Kolmstun.

OSKAR *crawls across the floor and hides. We can still see his face.*

Hello.

He opens the door, with a heavy push the door opens, OSKAR *winces.*

Hello?

HALMBERG *gets out his police baton. He carefully walks into the apartment.* OSKAR *hears him do so.* HALMBERG *walks around the table, he doesn't notice* OSKAR, *he opens the curtains, light spills in.*

OSKAR *takes his knife from out of his trousers. He looks at the blade.*

Hello? Is no one here…

HALMBERG *carefully approaches the trunk.* OSKAR *rolls out from out of the sofa.*

HALMBERG *tries the trunk. It doesn't budge. He tries it again. He puts his back into it. The trunk opens.* OSKAR *rolls out from under the table. He stands.*

Fucking hell.

HALMBERG *looks horrified at what's inside the trunk. A body. He softly takes* ELI's *hand. He feels for a pulse. There is no pulse.*

OSKAR *realises it's now or never – he clears his throat.*

HALMBERG *turns and looks at* OSKAR. *And then at the knife.*

What the fuck do you think you're doing?

Suddenly ELI *jumps onto* HALMBERG's *back. She sinks her teeth into his neck. He screams out. So does she. There is smoke coming from her.*

HALMBERG *tries to fight back, but falls to the floor. She pulls him inside the trunk.*

There is a moment's silence. OSKAR *– entirely bewildered, shocked and appalled – sits.*

There is the sound of drinking.

OSKAR *just listens to it.*

ELI. Shut the door, Oskar.

OSKAR *sits where he is.*

Shut the door, Oskar.

OSKAR *stands and shuts the door. And then returns to where he was sitting.*

ELI *joins him. Blood running down her chin.*

You saved me.

OSKAR *says nothing.*

I'm going to have to go now.

A tear rolls down OSKAR's *face.*

I can't stay here now. There'll be others that will follow him.

She reaches out and touches OSKAR's *face. She takes the tear from his cheek.*

You did the right thing. He would have killed me. Or the light – would have.

She puts the tear in her mouth.

I'm sorry, Oskar. I'm really sorry.

Neither say anything for what seems like for ever.

I'll be gone by tomorrow. I have no choice.

OSKAR. But – I – don't want you to go…

OSKAR *begins to cry.*

ELI. Don't you understand? I don't want to go either. But I have no choice.

She touches his face.

I see you, Oskar. You will be strong without me.

OSKAR. I could come with you.

ELI. No. You couldn't.

She touches his hair.

Promise me, when I'm gone. You'll let the light in.

OSKAR. Let the light in?

ELI. Promise me.

Promise me and forgive me.

Scene Twelve

OSKAR *is somehow alone.*

Immediately alone.

The world seems bleak without her. And he is bleak within the world.

He sits and puzzles with his Rubik's Cube.

But nothing can take the ache away.

Scene Thirteen

Around OSKAR *the sweet shop grows. A world of sweets that now seem strangely alien.*

OSKAR *stands in the sweet shop.*

He's not sure what to do.

KURT. Back again, son…

OSKAR *looks up at him blankly.*

OSKAR. Only for some monkeying around…

KURT. Yes. I remember your friend. Can I get you something?

OSKAR. I'll have some monkey – fur.

KURT. I don't stock monkey fur, son.

OSKAR. No. I don't mean monkey fur… I mean, something funnier. I'll have some – bananas – some peanuts.

KURT. I've got chocolate peanuts.

OSKAR. You look like a monkey.

KURT *looks at him a moment. Sad.*

KURT. Does it make you feel good telling me that?

OSKAR. No.

KURT. Maybe you should get out of my shop, eh?

OSKAR. Okay.

Scene Fourteen

OSKAR *knocks on the wall.*

'E–L–I.'

He knocks again.

'E–L–I.'

He opens the window and looks out.

He realises she's not coming.

He realises she's gone.

Scene Fifteen

OSKAR *sits on the jungle gym.*

He takes out his Rubik's Cube.

He looks at it.

He begins to rearrange it.

He rearranges the pieces in the perfect Rubik's Cube.

In the background MICKE *appears – he looks at* OSKAR, *frowns, and then softly approaches him.*

MICKE. Oskar…

OSKAR *turns and looks at* MICKE.

OSKAR. You haven't used that name in a long time.

MICKE. Not so long.

OSKAR *looks at him.*

OSKAR. What do you want?

MICKE. You haven't been to strength-training in a while.

OSKAR. Maybe I decided I was strong enough.

MICKE. Aye?

OSKAR. Yup.

Beat. MICKE *thinks. He smiles.*

MICKE. You remember that time at camp when we hooked up that rope water slide?

OSKAR. I slipped and gave myself a rope burn.

MICKE. Good though, wasn't it?

OSKAR *considers.*

OSKAR. Yes.

MICKE. I liked that summer, a lot.

OSKAR. Did you?

MICKE. Yes.

OSKAR *checks* MICKE*'s face.*

OSKAR. Me too.

Pause.

Micke…

MICKE. I can't stay. Got to get home. I just wanted to say: you should come again. To strength-training.

OSKAR *looks at him, he scratches his nose.*

OSKAR. Maybe I will.

MICKE. Bye, Oskar.

OSKAR *looks after him – faintly astonished.*

OSKAR. Bye. Micke.

Scene Sixteen

OSKAR *sits back in the changing room.*

He gets changed into his swimming costume. He doesn't cover himself up much as he does. It's as brave as he gets.

MR AVILA *enters the changing room. He smiles when he sees* OSKAR.

MR AVILA. You're back.

OSKAR. I am.

MR AVILA. It's good to see you again.

OSKAR. A man faces up to his troubles.

MR AVILA *thinks and then sits beside* OSKAR.

MR AVILA. I thought a lot about what you said – about how I could have done more to – help you.

OSKAR. I'm sorry I said that.

MR AVILA. I heard you wrote Jonny a note. That was a good thing to do.

OSKAR. I've decided to try and do good things.

MR AVILA *looks at* OSKAR.

MR AVILA. You're early tonight. It's nice to see.

OSKAR. I had nowhere else to be.

MR AVILA. Get some early lengths in. I'll be in when the others arrive.

OSKAR. Okay.

OSKAR *exits for the swimming pool.*

MR AVILA *watches him exit. He rubs his face – worried.*

MICKE *enters. He looks at* MR AVILA.

MICKE. Hello, Mr Avila.

MR AVILA. Hello, Micke.

MICKE. Was that Oskar I saw?

MR AVILA. I don't want any trouble.

MICKE. Okay.

He nods off. JONNY *enters. Followed by a seventeen- to eighteen-year-old guy,* JIMMY.

MR AVILA. Hello, Jonny. Who's this?

JIMMY. Jimmy, sir, Jonny's brother, you used to teach me.

MR AVILA. Yes. Jimmy. Of course. You've got bigger. But I'm sorry to tell you – I'm afraid this session is the junior swim.

JIMMY. I'm not here for the session, sir.

MR AVILA. You here to check Jonny will be okay? It's okay. We've been told the stitches will hold in the water. It might even be good for him.

JIMMY *firmly headbutts* MR AVILA. *Who crumples down. He hits him again.*

JIMMY. I'm not here for that either.

He looks at MR AVILA. *He bends down and gets some keys from his waist. He throws them to* MICKE.

I want every door locked.

JONNY. Jimmy…

JIMMY *stands to full length above his little brother.*

JIMMY. You going to be a little cunt?

He slaps JONNY *on the bad ear.*

JONNY. No.

JIMMY. You going to be a little cunt?

He slaps him again.

JONNY. Ow. No.

JIMMY. I told you, Jonny. No one hurts my brother and gets away with it.

Scene Seventeen

OSKAR *swims lengths alone in the pool.*

He's not the greatest swimmer. And he doesn't like getting his hair wet.

MICKE *is the first one into the pool area.* OSKAR *frowns at him.*

OSKAR. Hello, Micke.

MICKE *says nothing.*

You're wearing shoes. Mr Avila doesn't like it when you wear shoes.

MICKE. Mr Avila isn't here.

JONNY *enters next.* OSKAR *frowns when he sees him.*

OSKAR. Hello, Jonny. You got my note?

JONNY. I got your note.

OSKAR. I'm really sorry about your ear. I hear it will get better.

JONNY. Do you think we're friends now, Piggy?

OSKAR. No.

JONNY. Piggy. I burnt your note.

OSKAR. What? Micke…

MICKE. Don't look at me.

JONNY. Piggy. There's someone I'd like you to meet…

JIMMY. You call him Piggy?

MICKE. Yes.

OSKAR. Micke…

JIMMY. Why? He's not fat.

MICKE. He squeals like a pig.

JIMMY. That right. Hello, Piggy. I'm Jimmy, Jonny's older brother.

OSKAR. Hello. I'm Oskar.

JIMMY. Oskar is it?

OSKAR. Yes.

JIMMY. Hello, Oskar. We're going to play a game.

OSKAR. Okay.

JIMMY. How good are you at holding your breath, Oskar?

OSKAR. I'm okay.

JIMMY. Okay. So here's the game. Jonny got given a new
digital watch by our fag of a stepfather for his birthday. He's
going to time you, you can work the timer, right, Jonny?

JONNY. Right.

JIMMY. He's going to time you. If you get over three minutes
then – when you come up – I will nick you…

OSKAR. Nick me?

JIMMY. With this knife.

He takes out a butterfly knife and flicks it elegantly open.

OSKAR. And if I don't get over three minutes…

JIMMY. Then I will stab you through the eye with it. An eye for
an ear.

OSKAR. But… I don't think I can get over three minutes.

JIMMY. Then I will help you.

*He grabs OSKAR's hair and twists him and pushes him into
the water…*

OSKAR. No… I…

*… and then pushes him under the water. And it's suddenly
deadly quiet.*

*We stay on OSKAR's face for what seems like too long. He is
desperately holding his breath.*

Around him, carnage rages.

First JIMMY, *then* JONNY *and then* MICKE *are pulled violently away from the pool's edge.*

They struggle desperately. But are overwhelmed.

They are murdered. Dispatched. ELI *is an efficient and brilliant killer.*

Because of course it is ELI *killing them.*

As our boys lie dead. Sprawled across the space, so she climbs up to the tank.

And OSKAR *opens his eyes and realises he's been saved.*

He emerges back into the light.

He looks around himself. He sees ELI. *And she sees him.*

They hold each other's gaze for a moment.

Your nose is bleeding.

ELI. No one invited me in.

OSKAR. You can come in.

ELI. Thank you.

OSKAR *smiles.*

OSKAR. I'm pleased you came.

ELI. Thank you.

The two smile at each other.

Scene Eighteen

OSKAR *is on a train. He sits as a beautiful landscape passes him by.*

He is alone. Except for a trunk at his feet. A conductor, STEFAN, *enters the carriage.*

OSKAR *holds out his ticket. The conductor punches it.*

STEFAN. You travelling alone?

OSKAR. Yes.

STEFAN. Is someone meeting you the other end?

OSKAR *shakes his head.*

OSKAR. No.

STEFAN *indicates the trunk.*

STEFAN. Isn't that a bit heavy?

OSKAR. It's not as heavy as it looks.

STEFAN. It's a pretty old-fashioned trunk. I haven't seen one like that in a while.

OSKAR. It was my grandfather's.

STEFAN. What have you got in there… If you don't mind me asking.

OSKAR. A little bit of everything.

STEFAN *frowns, and then thinks, and then nods to himself.*

STEFAN. Okay, well, if you need anything…

OSKAR. Thank you.

STEFAN. Have a good trip.

He exits. OSKAR *is left. He knocks on the top of his trunk.*

'I L–O–V–E Y–O–U.'

The box knocks back.

'G–O–O–D.'

OSKAR *smiles.*